B53 029 152 6

D1464472

A Day in the Life: Polar Animals

Polar Bear

Katie Marsico

Raintree

www.raintreepublishers.co.uk
Visit our website to find out
more information about
Raintree books.

To order:
☎ Phone 0845 6044371
🖷 Fax +44 (0) 1865 312263
✉ Email myorders@raintreepublishers.co.uk

Customers from outside the UK please telephone +44 1865 312262

Raintree is an imprint of Capstone Global Library Limited,
a company incorporated in England and Wales having its
registered office at 7 Pilgrim Street, London, EC4V 6LB
– Registered company number: 6695582

Text © Capstone Global Library Limited 2012
First published in hardback in 2012
First published in paperback in 2013
The moral rights of the proprietor have been asserted.

All rights reserved. No part of this publication may be
reproduced in any form or by any means (including
photocopying or storing it in any medium by electronic
means and whether or not transiently or incidentally to some
other use of this publication) without the written permission of
the copyright owner, except in accordance with the provisions
of the Copyright, Designs and Patents Act 1988 or under the
terms of a licence issued by the Copyright Licensing Agency,
Saffron House, 6–10 Kirby Street, London EC1N 8TS (www.
cla.co.uk). Applications for the copyright owner's written
permission should be addressed to the publisher.

Edited by Daniel Nunn, Rebecca Rissman, and Sian Smith
Designed by Joanna Hinton-Malivoire
Picture research by Hannah Taylor
Original illustrations © Capstone Global Library
Production by Victoria Fitzgerald
Originated by Capstone Global Library Ltd
Printed and bound in China by South China Printing
Company Ltd

ISBN 978 1 406 22881 6 (hardback)
15 14 13 12 11
10 9 8 7 6 5 4 3 2 1

ISBN 978 1 406 22888 5 (paperback)
16 15 14 13 12
10 9 8 7 6 5 4 3 2 1

British Library Cataloguing in Publication Data

Marsico, Katie, 1980-
    Polar bear. -- (A day in the life. Polar animals)
    1. Polar bear--Juvenile literature.
    I. Title II. Series
    599.7'86-dc22

Acknowledgements

We would like to thank the following for permission to
reproduce photographs: Alamy Images p. 21 (© Stuart
Yates); Corbis pp. 4, 23c (Richard Berry/Design Pics), 14
(Chris Rainier); FLPA p. 7 (Minden Pictures/Flip Nicklin);
Getty Images p. 6 (Daniel J. Cox); Photolibrary pp. 5 (Oxford
Scientific/ Roland Mayr), 15 (Oxford Scientific/Eric LeFranc),
17 (imagebroker/ Jorn Friedrich), 18 (Imagebroker RF),
20 (Picture Press/Thorsten Milse); Shutterstock pp. 8 (©
Witold Kaszkin), 9, 23b (© Andy Farrer), 10 (© Lilyana
Vynogradova), 11, 23a (© Nik Niklz), 12 (©Gentoo
Multimedia Ltd.), 13, 23g (© Keith Levit), 16 (© Witold
Kaszkin), 19, 23d (© littlesam), 22 (© Witold Kaszkin), 23f (©
Danicek).

Cover photograph of a polar bear (Ursus maritimus) in
Spitsbergen, Svalbard, Norway reproduced with permission
of Photolibrary (age fotostock/ Morales Morales). Back cover
photographs reproduced with permission of Shutterstock: nose
(© Witold Kaszkin),
snow pit (© littlesam).

The publisher would like to thank Michael Bright for his
assistance in the preparation of this book.

Every effort has been made to contact copyright holders
of material reproduced in this book. Any omissions will
be rectified in subsequent printings if notice is given to the
publisher.

Disclaimer

All the Internet addresses (URLs) given in this book were valid
at the time of going to press. However, due to the dynamic
nature of the Internet, some addresses may have changed
or ceased to exist since publication. While the author and
publishers regret any inconvenience this may cause readers, no
responsibility for any such changes can be accepted by either
the author or the publishers.

Contents

What is a polar bear?. 4

What do polar bears look like? 6

Where do polar bears live? 8

What do polar bears do in the day?. . . 10

What do polar bears eat? 12

What threatens polar bears? 14

Do polar bears live in groups? 16

What do polar bears do at night? 18

What are baby polar bears like? 20

Polar bear body map 22

Glossary. 23

Find out more 24

Index 24

Some words are shown in bold, **like this**.
You can find them in the glossary on page 23.

What is a polar bear?

Polar bears are large **mammals** that live near snow and ice.

Mammals have hair and feed their babies milk.

Polar bears are powerful and skilled hunters.

They are **predators** in many **polar** areas.

What do polar bears look like?

Polar bears are some of the biggest bears on Earth.

These huge **predators** are very strong and have 42 sharp teeth.

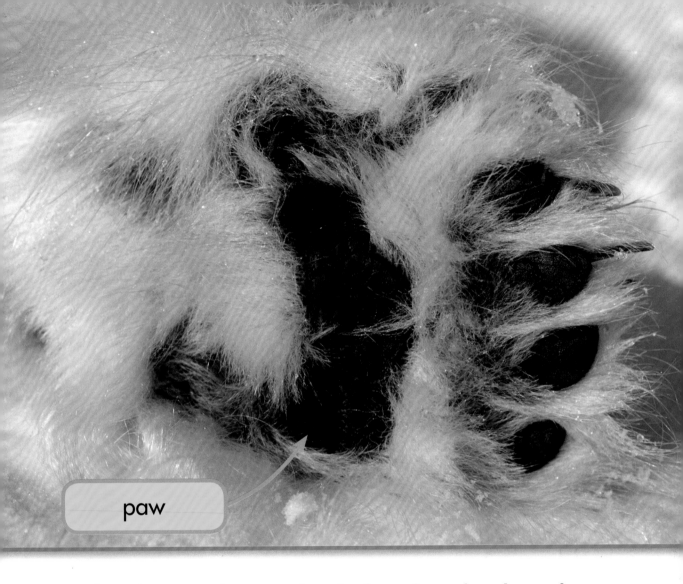

paw

Polar bears have thick fur that looks white and keeps them warm.

They even have furry paws that help them walk on ice and snow.

Where do polar bears live?

Arctic

Polar bears live in the **Arctic**.

In the Arctic it is light all day and all night for part of the summer.

In the Arctic it is dark all day and all night for part of the winter.

This **polar** area is one of the coldest places on Earth!

What do polar bears do in the day?

In midsummer, polar bears are most **active** in the morning and early afternoon.

They wake up after sleeping on ice or in snow **pits**.

pack ice

Polar bears spend part of the day hunting for food.

They catch a lot of their food around moving ice called pack ice.

What do polar bears eat?

seal

Polar bears use their strong sense of smell to hunt seals.

They also eat dead whales and walruses that wash up near the shore.

Polar bears will feed on almost anything.

This includes everything from reindeer and birds, to berries and rubbish!

What threatens polar bears?

Polar bears are the top **Arctic predators**, so most animals do not threaten them.

Killer whales and humans are their main enemies.

Pollution is a serious threat to polar bears, because it causes rising temperatures.

This leads to melting ice which endangers the food and homes of polar bears.

Do polar bears live in groups?

Polar bears do not usually live in groups.

These **mammals** spend much of their time alone.

Sometimes a small group of polar bears feed together in the same area.

Mother polar bears also live with their babies for one to three years.

What do polar bears do at night?

Polar bears spend quite a lot of time resting, both in the day and at night.

In midsummer, polar bears often sleep or rest near the end of the day.

Polar bears sleep for about seven or eight hours, similar to humans.

Many curl up and nap in snow **pits** or on blocks of ice.

What are baby polar bears like?

Baby polar bears are called cubs.

A mother polar bear usually gives birth to two cubs at a time.

The helpless babies grow bigger as they drink their mother's milk.

The cubs learn how to hunt and survive on their own in just 18 to 30 months!

Polar bear body map

nose

fur

mouth

paw

Glossary

active busy doing lots of things

Arctic area surrounding the North Pole. It is very cold in the Arctic.

mammal animal that feeds its babies milk. All mammals have some hair or fur on their bodies.

pit large hole

polar extremely cold areas at the top and bottom of the world

pollution harmful dirt, waste gases or chemicals, that damage the environment

predator animal that hunts and kills other animals for food

Find out more

Books

Arctic and Antarctic (Eye Wonder), Lorie Mack (DK Publishing, 2006)
Where Do Polar Bears Live?, Sarah Thomson. (Collins, 2010).

Websites

www.kidzone.ws/sg/polarbear/polar_bear.htm
Learn about where polar bears live and find out all about them on this website.

www.kids.nationalgeographic.com/kids/animals/creaturefeature/polar-bear/
Watch a video on polar bears and discover polar bear facts on the National Geographic website.

Index

Arctic 8, 9, 14
enemies 14
feeding 11, 12, 13, 17
fur 7, 22
groups 16, 17
mammal 4, 16
paws 7, 22
polar 5
pollution 15
predator 5, 6, 14
rest 10, 18, 19
size 6
snow pits 10, 19
young 4, 17, 20, 21